The Text of the Controversial
Republican White Paper

THE WAR
IN VIETNAM

Prepared by the Staff of the
Senate Republican Policy Committee

Public Affairs Press, Washington, D. C.

$1

THE WAR
IN VIETNAM

Prepared by the Staff of the
Senate Republican Policy Committee

Public Affairs Press, Washington, D. C.

Publisher's Note, Copyright, 1967, Public Affairs Press
419 New Jersey Avenue, S.E., Washington, D.C. 20003

Library of Congress Catalog Card No. 67-26288
Printed in the United States of America

PUBLISHER'S NOTE

Despite efforts to limit its availability to the public, the text of the controversial document prepared by the staff of the Senate Republican Policy Committee is published herewith in its entirety.

Since the report was initially intended for confidential consideration by Republican members of the Senate, only several hundred copies were mimeographed. To all indications additional copies were later to be widely distributed through party channels, but their availability was discontinued after a burst of newspaper publicity early in May.

The study appears to have had its origin in a proposal by Senator Jacob K. Javits (New York) to a meeting of the Senate Republican Conference on March 14, 1967. The first step toward forming a common position for Republicans on the war in Vietnam, Senator Javits suggested, might be a study by experts of the origin and nature of American commitments in that section of Southeast Asia. Senator Bourke B. Hickenlooper (Iowa), Chairman of the Senate Republican Policy Committee, then recommended that such a report be drawn up by the members of his group's staff — publicly-paid Congressional employees responsible to the Republican Senate leadership. The Javits proposal was unanimously approved by the 36 Republican Senators.

In the next five weeks, the members of the Policy Committee staff, working under the direction of Fred B. Rhodes, Jr., prepared this document.[1] Rhodes, the staff director, is a veteran legislative employee, having served on the staffs of the Armed Services, Joint Atomic Energy, and Appropriations Committees before becoming associated with the Republican Policy Committee in 1965.

Copies of the report were distributed to the 36 Republican Senators on April 26th with an injunction that its contents were not to be divulged until approved by the Senate Republican Conference. By April 28th, however, Senator Hickenlooper, fearful of a "leak"

---

1. In the course of drafting the report, the staff drew chiefly on transcripts of Congressional hearings, State Department publications, a "white paper" on Vietnam first published in 1965 and revised in September 1966 by the Committee on Planning and Research of the Republican Conference in the House of Representatives, and newspaper accounts of the war.

of its contents in distorted form, decided to issue copies to newsmen. After discussing his decision with Senators Javits and Margaret Chase Smith (Maine), the chairman of the Republican Conference, both of whom concurred, copies were released to the press, embargoed for publicity in newspapers of May 2nd, the day of the next scheduled meeting of Republican Senators.

Although many Senate Republicans hastened to point out that the document did not signify a shift away from G.O.P. support of the Johnson administration policies vis-a-vis Vietnam, few criticized the report as such or challenged its facts.[2] Nor did any quarrel with its exoneration of the Eisenhower administration from responsibility for the present situation.

Nevertheless, questions posed by the report, particularly in its conclusions, attracted so much attention and concern that Senate Republican leader Everett M. Dirksen (Illinois), who had been recuperating from pneumonia in Walter Reed Army Hospital, came to the May 2nd meeting with a statement in which he rejected what he considered misinterpretations of the report, but praised it as "a complete, authentic, well-documented, historical report on our involvement in Vietnam, a recital of Republican positions in the past, and two basic questions concerning the party commitments in the future."

Speaking for what Senator Hickenlooper called the "general consensus" of Republican Senators, Senator Dirksen added: "Preserving wholly the right of full and fair inquiry and criticism, we reiterate our wholehearted support of the Commander-in-Chief of our armed forces. We reaffirm our position of standing four-square behind him and our field, air and sea commanders in Southeast Asia as, with our superb fighting men, they fight to win this struggle against Communist aggression."

The next day, Senator Dirksen's counterpart on the other side of the Capitol, House Republican leader Gerald R. Ford (Michigan),

---

2. Senator John G. Tower (Texas), was almost alone in criticizing both the timing and contents of the report. In his judgment, issuance of the document "in the wake of a popularly acclaimed appearance by our top field commander in Vietnam" was "a classic political mistake." He referred, of course, to the appearance before Congress of General William C. Westmoreland. The Texas legislator also sent Senator Hickenlooper a memoraundum listing 23 interpretative and factual statements where he dissented from the language of the staff study. Senators Jack Miller (Iowa) and Karl Mundt (South Dakota) joined Tower in urging Republican insistence on sterner military action in Vietnam.

endorsed the above quoted words, emphasizing that the "overwhelming majority" of House Republicans agree that "we're not going to throw Vietnam into the political arena."

While the comments of Senator Dirksen and Representative Ford undoubtedly reflected the views of many Republicans, there were dissenters in the G.O.P. ranks.

On the day the report was made public, Senator George D. Aiken (Vermont), the Senate's senior Republican, delivered a statement in which he declared: "The significance for the Republican Party of this brief analysis is that American policy in Asia requires a new look — a fresh appraisal which can only come from a Republican administration."

Acknowledging that "there is almost as much divergence of view among prominent Republicans as among prominent Democrats," Aiken added: "The Vietnam conflict has split this country to a depth and with an intensity not experienced within this century. I know the President wants to bring this conflict to an honorable end. So do I. But the President predicates peace on the capitulation of the enemy and that solution seems far in the distance, if at all . . . This administration is too bound by its own vague criteria, its own predictions, its own predilections, its own conceptions and emotional commitments, to see the interest of the nation except in terms of its own survival as the government in power. . . ."

Two other prominent Republican Senators — Mark O. Hatfield (Oregon)[3] and John Sherman Cooper (Kentucky), joined Aiken in urging continued search for alternatives to a continuation of the war. Somewhat similar views were expressed by Senators Javits, Hugh D. Scott (Pennsylvania), and Charles H. Percy (Illinois).

Democratic legislators also were drawn into the debate. Predictably, those critical of the war's escalation hailed the report as evidence of dissatisfaction with the administration's policies. Senator J. William Fulbright (Arkansas), Chairman of the Senate Foreign Relations Committee and leading critic of the war, commended Aiken and urged that the report be distributed throughout the

3. "Republicans may not all share the same view concerning the war in Vietnam," Senator Hatfield declared, "but they will all respect and welcome the truth. This well written and carefully researched paper will, hopefully, invite a frank review within the Republican Party of this nation's policies and objectives in Vietnam. I believe this report will be of great value to us in proposing alternatives to administration policies which have been unable to bring either victory or solution."

country because he considered it the "most fruitful" development in the Vietnam debate in many months.

Speaking for Democratic legislators who support the administration's Vietnam policy, Senator John Stennis (Mississippi), Chairman of the Senate Preparedness Subcommittee, was critical of the report as a "trial balloon . . . in next year's presidential campaign" and warned that "under no circumstances should this war be made a political football by any group or either political party . . . We simply cannot afford to stop in the midst of a shooting war and debate whether we have been wise or unwise and whether our past actions were sound or unsound."

Judging by these varying views, the concern evoked, and the extraordinary amount of attention focused on "The War in Vietnam", this report[4] is clearly destined to become a central document in the continuing discussion within and between the two parties, and among the American people generally, concerning this nation's policy in Southeast Asia.

---

4. Except for minor changes, the phrasing of the chapter and sub-chapter headings is the same as that in the mimeographed version of "The War in Vietnam."

CONTENTS

1

DIMENSIONS OF THE WAR

As of April 1967, the war to contain Communist aggression in Vietnam has assumed for the United States these unusual dimensions:

- It means a conflict that has escalated from a small force of 600 American technicians to over a half-million fighting men.
- It means over 8,000 men killed.
- It means over 50,000 wounded.
- It means greatly increased American conscription at a time when the rest of the Western world has done away with its draft.
- It means our longest war since the American Revolution—six years—a weary nightmare and yet the men who fight are fighting with extraordinary bravery and skill.
- It means not knowing at any given moment precisely who the enemy is.
- It means a war which is not simply fought over this tiny land of Vietnam; for this war, unlike all others in American history, is more and more justified as much on geopolitical grounds as on the defense of one small government.
- It means our relative isolation as the world's policeman, for here we have no Grand Alliance as in World War II, no United Nations Combined Forces as in Korea. In addition to South Vietnamese troops, four Pacific nations have provided some fighting help —with our financial assistance.
- It means fighting a people who claim this is a civil war, and who in turn are spurred on by two giant powers quarreling openly with each other.
- It means that while we have committed 500,000 men to battle communism, neither the Soviet Union nor Red China—the great Communist powers—has found it necessary to commit troops.
- It means the most frustrating sort of war, with no front lines, which breaks out here and there, even across national borders in Laos and Cambodia, neither of which is involved.
- It means spending over $300,000 to kill each enemy soldier.

- It means spending $24 billion a year, with another increase in taxes threatened, a further drain on an already inadequate gold supply, and an escalation of inflation.
- It means enormous discretionary powers assumed by the President, with Congress asked to approve his actions after the fact.
- It means the nation which started the war—France and lost it, now has become our most outspoken critic while profiting heavily from the war.
- It means a war where, in the eyes of many Asiatics, we are fighting against indigenous Asiatic nationalism, much as France did in the past.
- It means the first war in our history fought not only on the battlefield but brought into the American livingroom, every day, through the raw emotionalism of today's mass communications.
- It means a war in which religious controversy between Catholic minority and Buddhist majority has come dangerously close to causing collapse of the successive governments of South Vietnam.

Here at home this confusion, this frustration, has raised challenges within Congress, within colleges and universities, within the press, within the military itself—and all to a degree not experienced in the United States since the Civil War. Conscientious objectors today outnumber their Korean counterparts 4 to 1.

2

BACKGROUND YEARS

Vietnam is a 2,000 year old country which, because of its exposed position, has been invaded by the Mongols, the Chinese, the Siamese, the French and the Japanese. One of the few things uniting the 30 million Vietnamese is a strong, common tradition of fighting outsiders.

The longest, most recent, most oppressive occupation—from the Vietnamese viewpoint—is still fresh in the minds of most Vietnamese. That occupation was by France; a white, western, capitalist, Christian power. America, no matter how pure its motives, cannot overcome the weight of history insofar as the Vietnamese look at it. In short, their memory of history is what we must learn to deal with, not our concept of it.

The most crucial moments in Vietnam's recent history came at the close of World War II, and are among the least remembered. The critical events of this era—the genesis of today's conflict—bear recounting in the strictest historical terms, complicated though they may be.

For nearly two decades prior to World War II, Vietnamese, directed in large measure by Ho Chi Minh, an exiled Communist from Annam, had carried on an underground struggle for independence from France.

Ho Chi Minh became the principal rallying agent for underground factions when the Japanese conquered Indochina during World War II.

The World War II pattern of Axis conquest, that of setting up local, native puppet regimes (Quisling in Norway, Laval in France) was broken in Indochina. The Japanese found a tractable colonial bureaucracy running the country, that of the Vichy French; they took advantage of it, and for a time allowed the French to continue doing business at the same stand, but with new directors. Not all the French in Indochina were so ready to cooperate. Many were secretly allied with the Free French under DeGaulle.

Both the United States and Nationalist China openly recognized Ho as leader of the free Indochina movement during World War II.

We supplied Ho's forces, the Vietminh, with arms and advisors.

Because of the Atlantic Charter and the outspoken United States stance in opposition to colonialism, the Vietminh and all Vietnamese had reason to expect U. S. support for their claim to independence following World War II. They had, after all, fought on our side—against both Japan and Vichy France.

Toward the end of the war, alarmed by the growing strength of the independence movement, Japan set up a puppet Vietnam government under the Emperor of Annam, Bao Dai.

Aftermath of Potsdam. The Potsdam Agreement provided that Chinese Nationalist troops were to disarm and intern Japanese forces north of the 16th parallel. British troops were to perform the same task in the south.

On September 2, 1945—following the Japanese collapse—Ho Chi Minh proclaimed from Hanoi the independence of all Vietnam. Bao Dai resigned, offered to serve the new government of independent Vietnam, and was appointed as an advisor.

British occupation forces, under Major General Douglas Gracey, put their own interpretation on the Potsdam Agreement and proceeded first to rearm, and then to use defeated Japanese troops to throw representatives of the newly proclaimed independent Vietnam government out of Saigon.

The consequences of this decision are with us today.

Thereafter, the British rearmed approximately 5,000 French troops interned in Saigon. On September 23, 1945, the British allowed the French *coup d'etat,* returning southern Vietnam to its colonial position under Paris' rule.

British and Japanese troops supported the French in battle against Vietnamese units until enough French reinforcements—50,000 of them—arrived by December of 1945 to reestablish total French domination in the south.

Commenting on the use of Japanese soldiers to reestablish European colonialism, General Douglas A. MacArthur is reported to have said: "If there is anything that makes my blood boil, it is to see our Allies in Indochina and Java deploying Japanese troops to reconquer the little people we promised to liberate. It is the most ignoble kind of betrayal."

An Eight-Year Colonial War. Thereafter began an eight-year colonial war which did not then attract general attention in the United States. We were deeply involved elsewhere.

We were, in 1946, attempting unsuccessfully to establish a modus vivendi with the Soviet Union. The Cold War had begun.

In 1947, through the Marshall Plan, we were trying to rebuild a shattered Europe. This same year we had to move with arms and men to yet another Cold War frontier, the Greek and Anatolian Peninsulas.

In 1948 one more Iron Curtain rang down—this time over Czechoslovakia—necessitating the establishment of NATO to defend the rest of free Europe from Communist aggression. A few months later we were in the grim struggle to save West Berlin—and West Germany—by means of the Berlin airlift.

As for Asia our attention was riveted on the war between Chinese Nationalists and Chinese Communists for control of mainland China. In terms of stakes in the Cold War, our commitments were elsewhere than Indochina. While we occasionally urged France to grant independence to these peoples—as we ourselves had already done for the Philippines—our prime concern was to secure French cooperation in forming NATO. Since France was absolutely vital to the success of the North Atlantic Treaty Alliance and was a permanent member of the U. N., we found it inappropriate to nudge France on the matter of colonialism in quite the same fashion as we did with the Netherlands in Java.

In 1949 the Communists had conquered mainland China, igniting a stormy debate within the United States. It was obvious that a nation of 3.7 million square miles, bursting with half a billion people, under aggressive Communist leadership, had to be contained. This containment of Chinese expansion was to become the key aspect of President Truman's Asia policy.

France argued that while Ho Chi Minh was admittedly the leader of Vietnamese nationalism, he was also a Communist. He was beginning to receive aid from Communist China. Therefore, the French were able to convince us that containment of China meant support of French colonialism in Vietnam.

France Recognizes Ho Chi Minh. Despite the "ignoble betrayal" referred to by General MacArthur, Ho Chi Minh found it convenient to negotiate with French representative Jean Sainteny. As a result of the agreement entered into, in March 1946, France recognized the

Republic of Vietnam as a "Free State" within the French Union, under Ho Chi Minh, with its capital at Hanoi.

In return, Ho Chi Minh agreed to the stationing of French troops in the north with the understanding they would be withdrawn by 1951. The French agreed to permit a referendum as to whether all of Vietnam would become a unified, independent state within the French Union.

France abided by neither promise. Troops were not withdrawn, nor were elections held. Instead, France took a step which was to insure 20 years of conflict—conflict which continues to this day.

On June 1, 1946, Admiral G. Thierry D'Argenlieu, the new French High Commissioner in Indochina, established and recognized a puppet government in South Vietnam.

The Vietnamese desire for independence was frustrated a second time. Subsequent negotiations proved fruitless. So intense by now was the Vietnamese hatred for France that Ho Chi Minh, a Communist, was able to crystallize these emotions into a willingness by many Vietnamese—whether Communist or not—to fight against the French occupation forces for eight years, eventually to win.

Gradually, Ho Chi Minh's forces won control of most of Vietnam. French power shrunk to control of forts and the few large cities. To bolster their collapsing government in Vietnam, France appealed to the one-time Japanese puppet Bao Dai to again become head of state.

Negotiations were begun with Bao Dai in 1948, finally resulting in the "Elysee" Agreements.' As ratified by the French Parliament in January 1950, the Agreements—278 pages of tendentious legalisms—created three "autonomous" states, Laos, Cambodia, and Vietnam. In these states, France retained control of foreign relations, armed forces, and, for all practical purposes, finances.

It was at this time, in January of 1950, that Ho Chi Minh sought and secured recognition from the Soviet Union and from Communist China.

On February 1, 1950, Secretary of State Acheson stated that the recognition by the U.S.S.R. and Communist China of Ho Chi Minh's government "should remove any illusions as to the 'Nationalist' nature of Ho Chi Minh's aims and reveals Ho in his true colors as the mortal enemy of native independence in Indo-China."

On February 7 both the United States and Britain recognized the Bao Dai Government.

In May Mr. Acheson announced the U.S. would provide aid to restore "security" and "develop genuine nationalism" in Indochina.

With the outbreak of the Korean War in June 1950, President Truman announced the "acceleration" of aid to Indochina.

It was argued in 1950 the decision by President Truman to assist the French in Indochina was a logical extension of the Truman Doctrine which evolved in the Mediterranean in 1947. Under that doctrine the United States had sent aid to Greece and Turkey when threatened with Communist aggression.

There were some basic differences between the Greek-Turkish situation and that found in Vietnam in 1950.

Greece was an independent nation with clearly established and defined borders, and an internationally recognized government. It was being attacked by Greek Communists who were based—and financed—from abroad. There was no popular internal revolution in process, no fight by the Greek people for freedom from foreign domination. The Greek government requested help. First Britain, then the U.S. responded with money, arms, and advisors.

Turkey was also a long-established nation with a recognized government whose borders were threatened by the Soviet Union. The government requested help and we responded with money, arms, and training advisors.

Vietnam was an altogether different situation. For the first time, we were officially committing American arms, money, military advisors to a colonial war on the side of colonial power.

The decision by President Truman was made in a peculiarly turbulent political climate. The fall of China had so charged the political atmosphere in Washington that the French appeal for assistance met readily receptive ears. The overt attack by the Communists in Korea, combined with the Communist recognition of Ho Chi Minh earlier in the year, seemed to justify even more the position adopted by the Truman administration.

In August of 1950, the first American military advisors arrived in Vietnam—35 of them.

From this point, all opponents of the Bao Dai government were labeled Communists by the French. The tragic, unintended result of this was, as President Eisenhower noted in his book, *Mandate for Change, The White House Years*: "had elections been held as of the time of the fighting, possibly 80 percent of the population would have voted for the Communist Ho Chi Minh as their leader, rather than Chief of State, Bao Dai. . . ."

The Eisenhower Inheritance. Aid received from Communist China beginning in 1950 had already enabled Ho Chi Minh's forces to capture one by one the entire French line of forts along the Chinese border. With the conclusion of the Korean War, Communist China was able to increase its aid to the Vietminh.

In 1953 President Eisenhower took office. He was forced to make basic decisions on Indochina almost at once. Most important was whether to continue assistance to the French, cut it back, or end it. President Eisenhower decided to continue and increase American aid, but to attempt to channel this aid around the French directly to Bao Dai and the Vietnamese people. He hoped to make Bao Dai more independent of France, more acceptable to the Vietnamese.

The French balked, insisting on keeping total control over all military and most economic aid. A relatively small program of direct aid to the Vietnamese continued, although it was resented by the French.

By 1954 our aid program had totaled over $1 billion. As the French military collapse accelerated, we were underwriting a high percentage of the cost of their war.

Troubled Spring. In January and February of 1954 a four power conference met to discuss the status of Berlin. Unable to resolve that question the representatives turned to other matters and agreed that a conference at Geneva would be convened in May to effect "a political settlement of the Korean question" and to discuss "the problem of restoring peace in Indochina." While not originally intended as a conference to settle boundaries in Indochina, but rather as a discussion of a cease fire, Ho Chi Minh's artillery was already at work writing a different conclusion. The saga of Dien Bien Phu had begun.

With the French military catastrophe at hand, President Eisenhower had to decide whether or not to intervene directly. The question of American intervention in Vietnam was put to the President on March 20, 1954, by the French Chief of Staff, General Paul Ely. He stated that only by massive American intervention could France hope to prevent a defeat at Dien Bien Phu. Without such intervention, it was intimated, France would be obliged to negotiate a settlement with the Vietminh.

In short, the general French thesis—supported by many Americans—seemed to be that if we did not intervene we would be handing the whole of Southeast Asia to the Communists.

A sharp argument arose within the Eisenhower administration. The Chairman of the Joint Chiefs of Staff, Admiral Arthur Radford, proposed a major United States military intervention from the sea beginning with air strikes to support the French at Dien Bien Phu. General Matthew Ridgway opposed this.

Congressional leaders were consulted.

President Eisenhower gave serious consideration to such proposals. However, he also circulated our allies in Europe and elsewhere as to the advisibility of and their willingness to join in such an intervention. He made clear that any intervention would have to be joint, not unilateral. Britain was the key, and refused, fearing it would scuttle the pending Geneva Conference and involve them in another endless colonial war.

Furthermore, France would not give satisfactory assurances, even at this late date, that it would grant independence to the peoples of Indochina.

In the end, President Eisenhower refused to permit a unilateral armed intervention to save a colonial regime. He declared that he could not "conceive of a greater tragedy for America than to get involved now in an all-out war in any of those regions [Indochina]."

The Eisenhower Approach. Several facts are worth noting. President Eisenhower, the professional military man, permitted a full, free debate over our Vietnam policy among military chiefs. In effect, it was General Ridgway arguing against the Chairman of the Joint Chiefs of Staff, Admiral Radford.

He also listened to Members of Congress who objected to American intervention in Vietnam.

Even though we had expended enormous amounts of aid in support of the French in Vietnam, President Eisenhower was willing to cash in his chips in 1954, no matter how humiliating it might be to admit we had backed a loser, rather than throw good blood after bad money.

In other words, he realized the application of military power could not resolve a hopeless political situation in Vietnam.

President Eisenhower had listened to all the arguments and weighed them carefully. Regardless of which individual advanced what argument, the ultimate decision was the President's. It was not the arguments that preceeded it, but the decision that counted.

The decision had the effect, as well, of cementing as an American position subscribed to by Republican and Democrat alike, at that time, that we should not become involved in another land war in Asia.

As a footnote to history, General Matthew B. Ridgway was to write in his memoirs: "when the day comes for me to face my Maker and account for my actions, the thing I would be most humbly proud of was the fact that I fought against, and perhaps contributed to preventing, the carrying out of some harebrained tactical schemes which would have cost the lives of some thousands of men. To that list of tragic accidents that fortunately never happened I would add the Indochina intervention."

The Geneva Conference. The Geneva Conference was not arranged to preside over the partition of Vietnam nor the withdrawal of France. Events at Dien Bien Phu—which fell on May 7, the day before the Vietnam phase of the Conference opened—dictated otherwise. The Conference did partition Vietnam and registered ultimate French withdrawal.

Participating in the Indochina phase were the United States, France, Britain and the Soviet Union, and after prolonged haggling, Communist China. These powers finally agreed that representatives of Cambodia and Laos take part along with a representative of Bao Dai and Ho Chi Minh.

The Conference was uniquely structured in that the five great powers were interested in an agreement on Indochina but were also interested in other problems and negotiations of equal delicacy. Indeed they may have considered the latter of greater importance than peace in Indochina.

The key was the European Defense Community. The U.S. and Britain were attempting to found EDC and felt they could not over-pressure France on the Indochina question. The Soviet Union was equally interested in blocking EDC and pressured Ho Chi Minh to make concessions to France which Ho did not feel were justified. Since the Vietminh controlled three-quarters of all Vietnam, Ho was confident he could quickly capture the rest. He also felt it was but a matter of time before Laos also fell to Communist rule. Communist China, at the time, was trying to present a more moderate image to the world and was willing to cooperate with the Soviet Union in forcing Ho Chi Minh to ease his demands.

During the Conference France underwent a domestic crisis because of military reverses in Indochina and elected a new Premier, and thus a new set of negotiators. Even so, France emerged from the Conference having salvaged at the negotiating table much of which she had lost on the battlefield.

Ho Chi Minh agreed to pull Vietminh forces out of South Vietnam, which they largely controlled, back above the 17th parallel.

The Conference agreed to withdrawal of "regular troops," but did not press the issue of guerrillas. There was to be only routine replacement of troops and armament. Reinforcement and introduction of new weapons were prohibited. The population was to be allowed to move freely from one zone to another. A special "regroupment area" was created in Laos for the Communist Pathet Lao, composed of the northern provinces bordering on China and North Vietnam.

On the subject of reunification of North and South Vietnam the Conference made it clear the 17th parallel was not to be a permanent dividing line. It called for nationwide elections within two years, by July 1956. This last provision was assented to orally by all parties except the U. S. and Bao Dai.

The International Control Commission was to supervise observance of all provisions including elections. The Commission was composed of India (chairman), Poland and Canada.

Neither the U. S. nor South Vietnam signed the agreements. The U. S., in a separate statement, declared it would refrain from disturbing the agreements. The Vietminh probably were persuaded to accept the agreement because they felt confident that in two years the elections would sweep them into power.

Principal gain of the Vietminh was international recognition of their control over what has since become known as North Vietnam.

France — the government and French citizens — emerged from Geneva with Vietnam no longer a drain on resources and manpower, but with their commercial interests intact in South Vietnam. They profited vastly from the American investment, both economic and military, all through this decade. They still profit today.

The New South Vietnam. With Vietnam divided—at least temporarily—as a result of the Geneva Conference, the Eisenhower administration was faced with yet another critical decision: whether to give aid to the government of South Vietnam.

During the Geneva Conference, Bao Dai had persuaded Ngo Dinh

Diem to become premier of his government. Diem was strongly nationalist, anti-French and anti-Communist. He was, however, an
unknown quantity, both in his homeland and internationally, as to
his ability to govern; many considered him a mere caretaker until
the 1956 elections when, they were confident, Ho Chi Minh would
come back to power.

The events of the next 18 months read like a history of the Byzan-
tine court. There were American officials—civil and military—who
supported Diem, and Americans who thought him inadequate. There
were French officials who actively conspired against him; others
actively cooperated. Bao Dai—"governing" from Paris or the Riviera
—alternately backed his premier, charged him with usurping his
power, demanded his resignation, or ordered Viet troops to fight in his
defense. Diem's army commander negotiated with the French, or
disaffected Vietnamese, to overthrow him.

Diem had no administrative corps upon which to draw, the French
were leaving and Vietnamese who had served under the French were
not welcome. Great areas of South Vietnam were governed by nearly
autonomous religious sects with their own armies. The Saigon police
were a Mafia-like group of gangsters—also with their own militia.

Compounding the confusion in Saigon, a million refugees from the
north fled Ho Chi Minh's Communist dictatorship and settled in
South Vietnam. Diem had to provide housing, employment and food
for the refugees and attempts to relocate them.

Ho Chi Minh used the two years 1954-56 to consolidate his power
in North Vietnam. No longer leading a band of guerrilas, he took
the course all newly-constituted Communist regimes have taken.
Those who opposed his rule were killed. At least 50,000, perhaps as
many as 100,000 were slaughtered. A peasant uprising was put down
brutally. Small landowners—many of them with only a tiny fraction
of an acre—were treated as though they were absentee landlords:
they were shot.

In short, the million who fled south were fleeing a reign of terror.

Diem: The Successful Years. Diem hung on. For the first time
there was a Vietnam independent of both France and the Communists. A group of officials within the Eisenhower administration
argued that this fact alone merited American support and aid. Addi-
tionally, they argued, such aid could now go directly to the Vietnamese people, in line with the original Eisenhower goal.

Thus, when Diem formally requested assistance from the United States—economic aid immediately to help care for the refugees as well as long-term aid programs—President Eisenhower agreed to help in a letter dated October 23, 1954.

That letter, so often trotted out by succeeding administrations to prove that whatever they did was simply in line with the Eisenhower "legacy," deserves to be quoted:

"I am accordingly instructing the American Ambassador . . . to examine with you in your capacity as Chief of Government, how an intelligent program of American aid given directly to your Government can serve to assist Vietnam in its present hour of trial, provided that your Government is prepared to give assurances as to the standards of performance it would be able to maintain in the event such aid is supplied.

"The purpose of this offer is to assist the Government of Vietnam in developing and maintaining a strong, viable state, capable of resisting attempted subversion or aggression through military means. The Government of the United States expects that this aid will be met by performance on the part of the Government of Vietnam in undertaking needed reforms. It hopes that such aid, combined with your own continuing efforts, will contribute effectively toward an independent Vietnam, endowed with a strong Government. Such a Government would, I hope, be so responsive to the nationalistic aspirations of its people, so enlightened in purpose and effective performance, that it will be respected both at home and abroad and discourage any who might wish to impose a foreign ideology on your free people."

There are several points worth noting with respect to this offer of aid.

The most important is that a primary condition was attached, and reiterated in several different ways, to wit, that the new government had to make the proper effort to survive on its own in order to receive economic and military assistance. This principle of "self help" on the part of the recipient country had long been advocated by Republicans.

The letter was primarily "political" in its prescriptions, emphasizing the establishment of a "strong," "viable" government, and the effecting of needed reforms in the country. The military program was intended to establish a climate of security to make the former possible.

A month previous, in September 1954, the SEATO agreement and
the Manila Pact had been agreed to by the U. S. and other nations,
specifically giving the states of Indochina a guarantee against aggression from the outside and subversion from within.

This, plus the promise of aid, had the immediate effect of giving
the Diem Government a combination of psychological, economic and
military support necessary for it to survive.

Diem, thereafter, moved first against the gangsters around Saigon,
and after defeating and dispersing them, disarmed and suppressed
the autonomous religious sects.   By October 1955, he felt strong
enough to propose a referendum between the absent Bao Dai and
himself. It was clear that Diem would have won overwhelmingly in
any event, but his brother felt it necessary to manipulate the election
giving Diem about 98 percent of the vote. This was the first indication that Diem's concept of a "viable" government was one in which
authority was centralized in the person of the President.

1956 Non-Election. The Geneva Agreements called for a national
plebiscite in Vietnam by July 1956. That election was never held.

Diem knew that were the election to be held, it would be a popu-
larity contest between himself and Ho Chi Minh; and he knew Ho
would quite likely win. Ho was far better known as the leader in
the fight against France. He had the aura of success about him.
On a head-count basis there were simply more votes to be cast in the
north than in South Vietnam. Further, Diem felt the International
Control Commission could not supervise the election properly in the
North and that Ho could as easily manipulate the polling there as
Diem had in his own election in 1955. Finally, France, which had
been commissioned at Geneva to help the ICC supervise the election
in the south had pulled out completely, early in 1955, at Diem's
insistence. The Geneva co-chairmen, Britain and Russia did not
name a replacement for the French.

So, Diem decided against allowing the election.

He defended his action by saying neither his Government nor the
United States had agreed at Geneva to the election and therefore
were not bound by that agreement, and that France, which had
agreed was gone. Technically, perhaps, he was correct. His decision
foreshadowed a renewal of guerrilla activity a year later, in 1957,
which became dangerously widespread and brutal in 1959-60.

Diem In Decline. Diem, by 1957, had taken other actions which made the renewal of revolutionary guerrilla warfare both inevitable and successful.

He suppressed all political opposition in the south, and not just the Viet Cong, but those who attempted to criticize him through the regular channels of parliament and press. His administration drew to a large extent from the Catholic refugees from the north, causing the beginnings of friction with the largely Buddhist population of the south.

Throughout history Vietnam's thousands of villages were traditionally governed by village chiefs or headmen. These village leaders had their family roots deep in the local soil, many having lived in the same village for centuries. Diem chose to replace many of these village headmen with appointees of his own from Saigon, causing deep resentment among the villagers so governed.

This resentment made it easier for the Viet Cong to draw much of its early support from non-Communist South Vietnamese. Many of the revolutionists in the South were not necessarily Communists to begin with, but rather anti-Saigon or anti-Diem.

The Eisenhower administration has been criticized for not pushing Diem harder on political "reforms.'" What is really meant is that Diem allowed the power structure he had so carefully put together in 1954-55 to disintegrate. To talk of superimposing western democratic institutions overnight on the Vietnamese culture is pointless. There exists no truly democratic nation from Burma to the gates of China in all of Southeast Asia.

A candid statement as to Diem's disintegrating regime, however, should not obscure one important point.

President Eisenhower stuck to his basic position that if there was a solution in South Vietnam, it was political and not military, insofar as the U. S. was concerned. That fundamental precept was not to be altered until 1961 when the new administration of President John F. Kennedy took office.

Thus, the Republican position could be summarized:

(1) No American armies in Asia, no land war in Asia;

(2) No commitment to aid colonialism or to suppress nationalism in Asia;

(3) In any event, no unilateral military intervention; a resort to force only under some international sanction, in particular the U.N.;

(4) Any multilateral commitment to force should be in a specific

area, for a specific, limited purpose in order to keep the conflict localized;

(5) Specifically in South Vietnam, the supplying of aid—money, supplies, arms—but not U. S. armies.

3

YEARS OF FAILURE

In 1961 President Kennedy had most of the same options President Eisenhower had in 1953; he could continue economic and military aid with the same emphasis on a political solution; he could increase aid, cut it, or phase it out. The choice was his.

We tend to forget the political climate of the time. The tone of the new administration was one of disdain for the performance of Eisenhower, particularly in the field of foreign affairs. There was a tendency in the Kennedy administration to believe that everything could be fixed if the proper American was sent there to fix it.

On April 30, in Vietnam, a group of 18 South Vietnamese leaders who had fought against the French signed an open letter to Diem demanding economic, administrative and military reforms. By November 11th anti-Diem feeling was so intense a military coup by elite paratroop battalions was attempted against the Diem regime. It failed.

One month later, in December 1960, the National Front for Liberation of South Vietnam (NLF) was formed by militant South Vietnamese insurgents—mostly Communists. Their platform was a renewal of open, armed warfare against the Saigon government, following 3 years of terror and assassination.

In dealing with the NLF, successive Democratic administrations have assumed since 1961 that the revival of the war in the South was undertaken solely at Hanoi's initiative. Secretary of State Dean Rusk says the war in the south "could end literally in 24 hours" if Hanoi so decided.

U. S. State Department assumptions that (1) South Vietnamese Communists are totally controlled by Hanoi, and (2) there is absolutely no difference between the ambitions of the two, are open to question.

It should be noted that the NLF has been southern oriented. Forty of their senior leaders were native South Vietnamese. The South Vietnamese Communists have, in the past, found Hanoi quite willing to enter into agreements at the expense of the South Vietnamese whether Communist or not. Examples:

One, on March 6, 1946, Ho Chi Minh entered into an agreement with the French which provided for a "free state" embracing what is now North Vietnam, but leaving southern Vietnam under French control.

Two, a second agreement on September 14, 1946, further confirmed Paris rule over the South Vietnamese.

Three, the Geneva Agreements of July 1954, left the south under control of the Diem government for at least 2 more years—this when most of the south was already under Communist control.

Four, thereafter, neither Hanoi nor Peking, nor Moscow made strong representations against dropping elections in 1956, in effect confirming Diem's control and leaving the South Vietnamese Communists out in the cold.

All of which is a reminder to the South Vietnamese Communists that North Vietnam has separate interests, and has not in the past been the most reliable of allies.

On January 29, 1961, Hanoi Radio recognized the NLF, praised it and shortly thereafter infiltration from North Vietnam into the south was stepped up. Terrorism was on the rise; assassinations of South Vietnamese increased; attacks on Diem military forces rose in number and ferocity.

President Kennedy, concerned with this increased Communist activity, told a news conference on May 5, 1961, use of American forces in South Vietnam was under consideration.

Thereafter, American counter-insurgency forces were moved into South Vietnam; President Kennedy reverted to old fashioned gunboat diplomacy and sent an aircraft carrier to demonstrate off Haiphong; troops were sent into Thailand and then withdrawn to show our strength and readiness to move.

From the vantage point of 1967 these maneuvers seem to have the thrust and feint of shadow boxing, but they were military actions and made more fateful military actions which were to follow much easier.

The Parade To Saigon. In 1961, too, began a parade of political, diplomatic and military figures from Washington to Saigon. May 11, six days after the President's press conference, Vice President Lyndon B. Johnson was dispatched to Southeast Asia. Warmed by a cordial, two-day session, Mr. Johnson likened President Diem to George Washington, Andrew Jackson, Woodrow Wilson, Franklin D. Roosevelt, and Winston Churchill.

In a joint statement at Saigon, May 13, Diem and Mr. Johnson said:

"The United States recognizes that the President of Vietnam, Ngo Dinh Diem, who was recently reelected to office by an overwhelming majority of his countrymen despite bitter Communist opposition, is in the vanguard of those leaders who stand for freedom on the periphery of the Communist empire in Asia."

On returning from Southeast Asia, Vice President Johnson wrote a memorandum to President Kennedy dated May 23, 1961: "The fundamental decision required of the United States—and time is of the greatest importance—is whether we are to attempt to meet the challenge of Communist expansion now in Southeast Asia by a major effort in support of the forces of freedom in the area or throw in the towel. This decision must be made in a full realization of the very heavy and continuing costs involved in terms of money, of effort, and of U. S. prestige. It must be made with the knowledge that at some point we may be faced with the further decision of whether we commit major U. S. forces to the area or cut our losses and withdraw should our efforts fail. We must remain master of this decision."

Close upon the Vice President's heels, Professor Eugene Staley of Stanford University visited Saigon for the administration. He was commissioned to direct an all-embracing study which was to form the basis for a new program of American aid.

Staley Strategic Hamlets. Staley prescribed large increases in the Vietnamese army, the Civil Guard and village militia, together with an increased flow of arms and radio communications equipment. Most of this equipment which went to the villages was later acquired by the Viet Cong.

The Staley plan also called for creation of the Strategic Hamlet, whereby scattered villagers would be brought together in compounds better to protect them from marauding Viet Cong. It was based on the successful British tactic in Malaya.

There were, however, basic differences between the British situation in Malaya a decade earlier and that found in Vietnam in 1961.

First, with the cooperation of the Thailand government, the British were able to seal the border and therefore deny the Communists in Malaya any overland supply routes.

Second, the Communist foe were largely Chinese aliens, squatters, and therefore readily identifiable.

Third, the native Malayan people were willing to cooperate because of the hostility with which they regarded these Chinese aliens. At most in Malaya the hard-core Communist terrorists numbered no more than 8,000 and the total Chinese population something over 400,000.

Fourth, the French had already tried it during their war in Vietnam and failed.

In Vietnam there could be no sealing off of the Laotian border which was controlled by Communists. Infiltration and cross-border movement were easy for the guerrillas. In Vietnam the Communist guerrillas were indigenous and could not be distinguished from non-Communist villagers. In Vietnam the villagers had lived on the same land for generations. They objected vehemently to being moved from their villages into what could too often be described as concentration camps. Finally, in Vietnam the guerrillas totaled between 15,000 and 20,000 armed men in 1961 and by 1962 this figure had grown to 30,000.

Yet, President Kennedy approved the program. On September 17, 1961, R. G. K. Thompson, former permanent Defense Secretary in Malaya, was brought to Vietnam in order to put the Staley plan into action.

The Taylor-Rostow Mission. On October 11, 1961, President Kennedy announced he was sending his military advisor, General Maxwell Taylor, and economist Walt W. Rostow, then the President's Deputy Assistant for National Security Affairs, to South Vietnam. Their mission was to find out "whether Vietnamese nationalism had turned irrevocably against us or still might serve as a basis for the fight against Communism."

It is generally agreed that the Taylor report contained not simply recommendations to beef up and improve military operations, but made a strong case for sweeping political reforms in the Diem government, including increased freedom of speech, some form of decentralization, and the release from jail of bona fide nationalist leaders.

Unfortunately, General Taylor's report was severely denounced by the government-controlled Saigon press for what it termed an attempt to infringe on South Vietnamese sovereignty. On November 24, 1961, the newspaper *Thoi-Bao* ran an eight-column headline: "Republic of Vietnam No Guinea Pig for Capitalist Imperialism—Is It Not Time to Revise Vietnamese-American Collaboration?" The accompanying article, echoed by other Saigon newspapers, contained accusations of American "interference" with internal affairs of South Vietnam, aimed at "gaining profits under the exploitation policy of capitalist imperialism." The Diem government refused to be swayed by broad diplomatic hints that we might recall our Ambassador if reforms were not effected.

The result was a joint American-Vietnamese eleven-point declaration of January 1962, which was clearly a compromise in favor of Saigon. The political reforms urged by Taylor were watered down, but military and economic support were increased.

The Qualitative Shift. The war in Vietnam—and American involvement—had taken a qualitative shift. By the end of 1961, it became apparent that the Kennedy administration had opted for military intervention.

Arthur Schlesinger admits that Mr. Kennedy's decision at the end of 1961 "was to place the main emphasis on the military effort."

The first American soldier was killed in open combat in 1961.

Perhaps the most succinct account of President Kennedy's decision to escalate the Vietnam conflict is that of his Assistant Secretary of State for Public Affairs, Robert Manning, who wrote in April 1967:

"One day late in 1961, President Kennedy discussed with his counselors a decision to increase the American 'presence in South Viet Nam from a few hundred 'military advisers' to a military force of 15,000 men. Undersecretary of State George Ball opposed this, arguing that it would seriously alter the character of the war and might eventually suck more than 300,000 American men into action there. Secretary of State Dean Rusk and Secretary of Defense Robert McNamara agreed that Ball's reservations were fair ones, but they were willing to risk the consequences. Kennedy decided that he was too.

"Hindsight marks that decision as a critical step in this country's creeping escalation toward international tragedy and a domestic crisis of politics and morality. Yet in the news reports of the day it was characterized only as a 'modest' increase in American advisory help to the beleaguered South Vietnamese government.

"What if news reporters had been told of the full discussion? They would have reported that the United States had decided to increase its commitment to 15,000 men, that this might lead to the involvement of as many as 300,000 soldiers—then unthinkable— and that the President's advisers disagreed about taking such a step. If the newsmen had told that story, how would the American public have reacted? Would the course of history have been changed?"*

The two principal historians of the Kennedy administration, Theodore Sorensen and Schlesinger, both plead that past American policy gave Mr. Kennedy virtually no alternative. Schlesinger states that President Kennedy, "had no choice now but to work within the situation he had inherited," and Dulles' policy in South Vietnam had "left us in 1961 no alternative but to continue the effort of 1954." Sorensen agreed.

Accepting this thesis at face value—that an entire Democratic administration was bereft of alternatives—pictures President Kennedy as a mere robot with no responsibility for whatever actions he took in Vietnam. Carried to its ultimate absurdity this thesis presents Lyndon Johnson as a captive of George Washington's policies, with no real justification for quadrennial Presidential elections.

U.S. Again Backs Diem. By February 7, 1962, the total of U.S. military personnel in South Vietnam had increased to 4,000. Three weeks later, two fighter planes piloted by members of the South Vietnam Air Force, bombed and strafed President Diem's Saigon palace. Diem's relations with American newsmen were deteriorating as correspondents for U.S. papers and networks were booted out of South Vietnam with increasing frequency. Yet the Kennedy administration, by the begin-

---

*NOTE: The historian searching for a motive in President Kennedy's decision to opt for a military solution in Vietnam finds two separate accounts.

The first is that of James Reston, *New York Times* editor: "A few minutes after this meeting [with Khrushchev in Vienna in June 1961] President Kennedy told me that apparently Khrushchev had decided that 'anybody stupid enough to get involved in that situation (the Bay of Pigs) was immature, and anybody who didn't see it thru was timid and, therefore, could be bullied.'" Mr. Reston says President Kennedy then put 12,000 American soldiers into Vietnam as an offset to Khrushchev's estimate of him, altho he was amply warned that he was creating an unlimited commitment and was violating all his pronouncements about not allowing the United States to get into an Asian land war. (*Washington Daily News*, June 2, 1966).

The second account is found in "Facing the Brink" by Edward Weintal and Charles Bartlett. "Had he not suffered reverses in the Bay of Pigs and Laos," they write, "it may well be that President Kennedy would have thought twice before expanding the Viet Nam commitment early in 1962 from 700 to 11,000 advisers. Had he followed a long-range policy plan rather than an understandable concern for his image as a result of the Bay of Pigs fiasco, he might have reduced rather than increased the Viet Nam commitment."

ning of March 1962, was attempting to rally public opinion behind
Diem. *Time* described it this way on February 23, 1962:

"Whatever the difficulties, the U.S. is sticking with Diem. Speaking
last week to Rotarians in Saigon, U.S. Ambassador Frederick Nolting
Jr. urged critics of Diem to be boosters instead of naysayers. 'The
divisions among patriotic, anti-Communist Vietnamese, which are no
secret to anyone here,' said Nolting, 'are in my judgment a great bar-
rier to your country's progress and a real danger to your country's
survival.' Conceding that Diem was taking his own sweet time in
instituting reforms, Nolting said that he agreed 'to a certain extent'
with those Vietnamese who complain that 'the real benefits of a free
society are not getting through to the people.' But he also praised
Diem's 'dedicated and courageous leadership,' added that reforms
'could be accomplished relatively quickly if only more people were
willing to work and sacrifice to accomplish them.' "

Washington soon after, according to *The New York Times*, in-
structed the American Mission in Saigon "to get along with President
Ngo Dinh Diem's regime come hell or high water and forget about
political reforms."

Lest the scale be tipped too far against Diem, it must be remembered the fabric of his regime was further weakened by acts of Communist terrorists. During 1962, an estimated 1,700 South Vietnamese
civilians were assassinated by the Viet Cong, frequently with unimag-
inable barbarism, and 9,688 were kidnapped. Their targets were not
just Diem's unpopular village administrators but school teachers, and
those engaged in agriculture and social reform; literally irreplaceable
citizens of South Vietnam.

Peking Proposal. On March 1, 1962, Secretary Rusk commented on
the request by Peking of February 24, 1962 that the co-chairmen of
the 1954 Geneva Conference, and other countries concerned, consult
regarding Vietnam. Said Rusk: "the United States is always prepared
to talk about situations which represent a threat to the peace, but
what must be talked about is the root of the trouble; in this case it is
the Communist aggression against Vietnam in disregard of the Geneva
Accords." No talks were held.

The Control Commission Report. On June 2, 1962, the Canadian
and Indian members of the International Control Commission in
Vietnam created by the 1954 Geneva Accords issued a report (which

Poland refused to sign) charging North Vietnam, South Vietnam, and the United States with factual violations of the Geneva Accord. Thereafter, the Commission issued no more reports until 1965.

U.S. Marines in Thailand. In 1961 The Three Princes War resumed in Laos. The U.S. had withdrawn its chips from the middle or "Neutral" Prince, and placed them on the "Rightist" Prince. His Royal Laotian Army suffered serious defections and reverses in 1962, and was driven by the Neutralist forces and Pathet Lao Communist forces across the Mekong River into Thailand. On May 15, 1962, at the request of Thailand, President Kennedy dispatched a force of 5,000 U.S. Marines into northern Thailand. On July 30, 1962, the Marines were withdrawn. Their effect on the outcome of the Geneva Conference on Laos was, at best, problematical.

The Conference convened in 1961, and finally achieved agreement in 1962. The agreement was billed by the Kennedy administration as neutralizing all of Laos. Actually it left untouched the Pathet Lao control of the Laotian territory bordering on Vietnam, through which North Vietnamese have been infiltrating to South Vietnam and supplying the Viet Cong.

About this time, in 1962, comforting analyses of the Vietnam conflict by two of the most prominent U.S. State Department officials were offered for public consumption, one as to the inferiority of the enemy and the other as to the limited nature of our commitment.

Said Under Secretary of State George W. Ball:

"The guerillas whom the Vietnamese Army is fighting are under distinct handicaps. In many cases they are poorly trained and equipped and not motivated by deep conviction. Rather, they are merely unsophisticated villagers or peasants who have been conscripted by terror or treachery. In such a case they are likely to have had only rudimentary training in weapons-handling and tactics. Their equipment may be makeshift, often just what they can capture or fabricate themselves.

"Only the leaders and the hard core have a strong ideological commitment. The rank and file are their puppets—those whom they have bought, coerced, or intimidated."

And Mr. Kennedy's roving ambassador Averell Harriman, in explaining why we could afford a military commitment in Vietnam but not Laos, said in 1962: "In Vietnam, on the other hand, a decision to assist the Republic of Vietnam to defend itself against the sort of attack being waged in that country would not involve the deployment of U.S. combat forces and would not require the occupation of foreign territory by the United States or other Western forces."

Political Developments in South Vietnam. On June 26, South Vietnam's National Assembly extended its own term of office by one year. And when on October 26, the Assembly extended Diem's emergency powers to rule by decree for another year, it was an act of near prophecy, for Diem was assassinated precisely one year and seven days thereafter.

In considering the politics of the Diem regime, it must be kept in mind that in Vietnam, as in most Asiatic countries, no tradition of formal representative government exists.

The Vietnam nationalist parties that formed during French rule were secret movements accustomed to operating clandestinely and often warring with each other. This tradition of secretiveness, of factionalism, of small, select groups composed of men who could be trusted implicitly, continues today.

Diem accomplished a miracle in putting together a stable government, and attracting support of many key factions of the elite in South Vietnam. If there is one point most observers agree on, it is that from 1958 onward Diem seemed to draw inward, losing touch with the coalition he had put together.

More and more, he appeared to rely on the advice of his immediate family and few others. Personal government, not new to Vietnam, was carried to an extreme.

Thus, when crack paratroop battalions surrounded his palace in 1960 and demanded reforms, their leaders were not thinking in terms of Western democracy; rather, they sought an end to deliberate use of the personal power of members of the Diem family to monitor the loyalty of civil and military officials, to control both the formulation and execution of policy, to determine who should be promoted in the civil and military bureaucracies, and to manipulate the military in such a way as to interfere with successful prosecution of the conflict with the Viet Cong.

While Communist pressure increased, Diem and his family devoted increasing attention to sumptuary legislation to improve Saigon morals. As an example of the state to which the National Assembly had been reduced, Madam Nhu—Diem's sister-in-law—was able to dictate legislation prohibiting men and women from dancing with each other .

Meanwhile, Viet Cong victories multiplied. On January 2, 1963, a force of 200 Viet Cong attacked and defeated a demoralized force of 2,000 South Vietnam regulars in the Mekong Delta. Five helicopters were shot down, killing three Americans.

By spring, military action was overshadowed by a series of tragic political events; yet administration pronouncements remained highly optimistic. In 1962 Defense Secretary McNamara had said, "Every quantitative measurement we have shows we're winning this war." On March 8, 1963, Secretary Rusk said the struggle against the Viet Cong was "turning an important corner" and concluded Diem's forces "clearly have the initiative in most areas of the country."

The Fall Of Diem. Of the near-million North Vietnamese who fled southward in 1954-55, roughly 90 percent were Catholic. It was among these people that Diem found many of his most loyal administrators. South Vietnam, predominantly non-Christian, found these refugees doubly alien. They were from the north; they were adherents of a Western religion. Whatever favoritism was shown northern Catholics by the Diem regime—and there is some evidence of such favoritism—created frictions and jealousies on the part of the leaders of the Buddhist majority.

On May 8, 1963, in the city of Hue, government troops fired into a crowd protesting Diem's strictures against flying the Buddhist flag during a religious festival.

Demonstrations spread to Saigon. On June 11, a monk committed suicide by setting fire to himself, to be followed in the next six months by six other acts of self-immolation.

On August 21, Diem's Special Forces attacked Buddhist pagodas in Saigon, Hue, and other cities, arresting a number of Buddhists.

Diem's Buddhist Foreign Secretary, Vu Van Mau, resigned in protest. Mme. Nhu's father, the Vietnamese Ambassador to the United States, also resigned along with most of his staff.

Students joined the Buddhist demonstrations. Diem closed the universities in Saigon and Hue, and all secondary schools in Saigon. About 4,000 students were arrested.

Not all opposition to Diem, his brother Nhu, and his sister-in-law, Mme. Nhu, arose from Buddhist leaders. Discontent in key segments of South Vietnam's rickety power structure was being transformed into rebellion.

Still, on July 11, 1963, Ambassador Nolting returned to Saigon from Washington with assurances of continued U.S. support of the government of President Diem. He called for "unity of purpose" and warned against "internal dissension."

Newspaper accounts describing the deteriorating situation in Vietnam had long been labeled propaganda by administration spokesmen. By the end of summer the Kennedy administration could no longer maintain the credence of the American people that Diem was popular with his own people and was winning the war. On September 2, 1963, in a CBS interview President Kennedy admitted Diem's regime had "gotten out of touch with the people" and that he believed it could regain support only if there were "changes in policy and perhaps with personnel."

On September 21, Secretary McNamara and General Taylor once again flew to Saigon. While they were there elections were held for the National Assembly. All candidates were approved in advance by the Diem government. Obviously, so far, no change in policy or personnel had taken place.

On October 2, 1963, the White House issued a summary of the McNamara-Taylor report on their findings. The summary makes interesting reading:

"Major U.S. assistance in support of this military effort is needed only until the insurgency has been suppressed or until the national security forces of the Government of South Vietnam are capable of suppressing it. Secretary McNamara and General Taylor reported their judgment that the major part of the U.S. military task can be completed by the end of 1965, although there may be a continuing requirement for a limited number of U.S. trained personnel. They reported that by the end of this year, the U.S. program for training Vietnamese should have progressed to the point where 1,000 U.S. military personnel assigned to South Vietnam can be withdrawn."

Added General Paul Harkins, Commander of the Military Assistance Command in Saigon, in the November 1, 1963 service newspaper *Stars and Stripes*: "Victory in the sense it would apply to this kind of war is just months away and the reduction of American advisors can begin any time now."

As *Stars and Stripes* was being delivered to the newstands that November 1, a military junta led by General Duong Van Minh, overthrew the Diem government and seized control of Saigon. The next day, November 2, Diem and his brother Nhu were assassinated.

Despite all the clamor, rioting, and discontent among civilians, in the end it was the South Vietnamese military—the group over which the U.S. had the greatest degree of direct control—which was to overthrow and assassinate Diem.

Political chaos was immediate in South Vietnam. Nonetheless, on November 15, a U.S. military spokesman carried on the McNamara-Taylor-Harkins line and promised 1,000 American military men would be withdrawn from Vietnam beginning on December 3.

On November 22, President John F. Kennedy was assassinated and a new President, Lyndon B. Johnson, took office.

Lyndon Johnson Takes Command. Once again a new American President had an opportunity to reassess the situation and the American position in Vietnam:

President Johnson could deal with an altogether new government in Saigon; he was not obliged to deal with the Diem family.

The NLF and Viet Cong controlled much of South Vietnam. By June of 1963, the NLF was able to levy taxes in 41 of South Vietnam's 44 provinces.

The NLF had already (reported by Radio Hanoi November 17, 1963) made a six-point peace statement, couched in violent accusatory language.

There were still fewer than 20,000 American troops committed to Vietnam.

According to *The New York Times,* UN Secretary General U Thant met with President Johnson shortly after President Kennedy's assassination and conveyed to him an offer from Ho Chi Minh proposing talks on a settlement.

President Johnson still had before him the DeGaulle offer on August 29, 1963, rejected by the Kennedy administration, to help work for an independent but neutral South Vietnam.

In December 1963, Cambodian Chief of State Norodom Sinahouk again invited South Vietnam to join his country in a neutral confederation.

While President Johnson had options to choose from, President Kennedy did not leave him the same alternatives which President Eisenhower left in 1961. Actions of the Kennedy administration had decidedly narrowed the field. The American commitment was greater; Americans were actually involved in combat; more and more, American military prestige was at stake.

In addition, President Johnson from all accounts was concerned with maintaining the appearance of continuity in both domestic and foreign policy.

In December 1963, President Johnson made his choice and announced it through his New Year's message to General Minh of South Vietnam. The message read in part:

". . . The United States will continue to furnish you and your people with the fullest measure of support in this bitter fight. We shall maintain in Vietnam American personnel and material as needed to assist you in achieving victory.

"Our aims are, I know, identical with yours: to enable your government to protect its people from the acts of terror perpetrated by Communist insurgents from the north. As the forces of your government become increasingly capable of dealing with this aggression, American military personnel in South Vietnam can be progressively withdrawn.

The "United States Government shares the view of your government that 'neutralization' of South Vietnam is unacceptable. As long as the Communist regime in North Vietnam persists in its aggressive policy, neutralization of South Vietnam would only be another name for a Communist takeover. Peace will return to your country just as soon as the authorities in Hanoi cease and desist from their terrorist aggression.

". . . I know from my own experience in Vietnam how warmly the Vietnamese people respond to a direct human approach and how they have hungered for this in their leaders. So again I pledge the energetic support of my country to your government and your people."

Thus President Johnson publicly revealed his belief that American involvement in Vietnam required an open-end military commitment.

The President now set the goal as military victory.

At a time when President Johnson was making his decision for deeper American involvement in Vietnam, the opportunity existed to make that involvement worthwhile by insisting on a sound civilian government in Saigon capable of leading the people. Yet, he allowed the military junta to continue its total dominance of the civilian government. The generals neither knew how to govern, nor showed any real desire to learn. The Administration, meanwhile, shipped in more money, more guns, and more American troops.

In the 18 months that followed ten governments passed through Saigon in quick succession, each more disorganized than the last.

The Johnson administration was to express high hopes for each of these ten regimes.   General Khanh, for instance—who replaced General Minh in January 1964—was described by McNamara as "an able and energetic leader," who has demonstrated his grasp of the basic elements—political, economic and psychological, as well as military—required to defeat the Viet Cong."   Etc., etc.

Khanh bounced in and out of the premiership for a year after the McNamara speech, finally was packed off as roving Ambassador to the world.

Despite this political chaos, when McNamara testified before Congress on February 18, 1964, he still insisted the "bulk" of U. S. troops would be pulled out by the end of 1965.

By July 1964, when General William C. Westmoreland succeeded to the command of the U. S. military advisory mission, our advisory body had grown to about 23,000, but the South Vietnamese whom they came to advise were melting away.   During the winter of 1964-65 the South Vietnamese Army had dwindled to slightly over 200,000 men.   They had lost by desertion, or to the Communists, a good third of their strength.

Not only was South Vietnam suffering from massive desertions from its army, but shortly after Diem's death it was discovered Staley's Strategic Hamlet Program was a crushing failure.   The U. S. Mission found thousands of supposedly "secure' hamlets were really controlled secretly by the Viet Cong, who often used them for supply and rest havens.   The United States had contributed tens of millions of dollars worth of equipment, including cement, radios, weapons, fertilizer and livestock.

When the Minh junta came into power Premier Tho stated that only 20 percent of the 8,600 Strategic Hamlets the Diem government claimed to have built could in any way be regarded as usable.

The succeeding military governments and juntas did little to remedy this situation.   The key to real security for the South Vietnamese peasant lay not so much in barbed wire but in the type of political leadership that would attract his loyalty and make the struggle against the Viet Cong seem worth the risk.

On March 26, 1964, Secretary McNamara admitted: "But the large indigenous support that the Viet Cong receives means that solutions must be as much political and economic as military.   Indeed, there can be no such thing as a purely 'military' solution to the war in South Vietnam."

The Presidential Election. At this point in history conduct of the affairs of Vietnam was once again influenced by political events elsewhere—the United States was involved in a presidential election campaign.

Through the summer of 1964, the Vietnam situation—both political and military—was deteriorating. Day-to-day conduct of the war remained the responsibility of Kennedy appointees who stayed with the Johnson administration. Rusk, McNamara, Bundy, Rostow, Taylor, were left to handle Vietnam while President Johnson electioneered.

The first indication of a theme that was to be struck repeatedly during the coming campaign was introduced during a television interview on March 15, 1964, when the President told the listening audience: "I was reading a letter only today that General Eisenhower wrote the late President Diem 10 years ago, and it is a letter that I could have well written to President Khanh and sent out by Mr. McNamara."

One of the most trying aspects of living with Mr. Johnson's conduct of foreign affairs is precisely this gambit which might be termed Diplomatic Darwinism. By this is meant the President's insistence that whatever he may be doing is but part of a steady evolution from commitments made by earlier Presidents, particulary President Eisenhower.

Thus, he was to reiterate during the presidential campaign that his several decisions by which we became engaged in a full-scale shooting war in Vietnam were merely logical implementations of that far away and long ago 1954 Eisenhower letter agreeing to limited aid for South Vietnam—money, supplies and arms, but not combat troops.

Gulf of Tonkin Resolution. A second justification, equalling the by-now tattered 1954 letter in usefulness, was the Gulf of Tonkin resolution of August 7, 1964. The series of events leading to the resolution began with a July 30th South Vietnamese naval raid on North Vietnamese island radar and naval installations. According to official accounts, the U. S. Seventh Fleet was not informed of the raid. On August 2nd a U. S. destroyer on patrol in the Gulf of Tonkin near the islands was attacked by North Vietnamese PT boats. The PT boats were driven off with gunfire and an air attack. The U. S. formally protested to Hanoi.

On August 4th two U. S. destroyers reported a second attack by

North Vietnamese PT boats. President Johnson ordered U. S. "air action" against "gunboats and certain supporting facilities in North Vietnam."

On August 5th President Johnson requested Congress to enact a joint resolution "to promote the maintenance of international peace and security in Southeast Asia."

Senator Jacob K. Javits (R., N. Y.) questioned the wisdom of such unilateral action on the part of the United States as provided for by this resolution. During consideration of the resolution he raised the same issue President Eisenhower had raised 10 years earlier when, in 1954, the French requested American assistance at Dien Bien Phu. In 1954 Mr. Eisenhower surveyed our allies as to their willingness to join in taking such a step.

Asked Senator Javits of Senator Fulbright in 1964: "What I wish to know from the Senator is, first: Have we consulted with our allies? Second, what are we to look to from our allies in the way of assistance, aid, comfort, partnership, and the future implementation of the resolution? It is one thing to stand alone; it is another thing to stand with seven other countries, three of them in the area, implementing a solemn commitment, which is just as binding on them as it is on us."

Scope of the Tonkin Resolution. The joint resolution was in three parts. The first expressed Congressional approval of the President's action to repel attacks on U. S. forces, and the third part extended the life of the resolution until the President should determine that peace had been restored or until terminated by concurrent resolution of Congress. These two sections were not challenged in the Senate debate.

Section 2, the center of discussion, reads: "The United States regards as vital to its national interest and to world peace the maintenance of international peace and security in southeast Asia. Consonant with the Constitution of the United States and the Charter of the United Nations and in accordance with its obligations under the Southeast Asia Collective Defense Treaty, the United States is, therefore, prepared, as the President determines, to take all necessary steps, including the use of armed force, to assist any member or protocol state of the Southeast Asia Collective Defense Treaty requesting assistance in defense for its freedom."

The potential effect of agreeing to this action was of concern to many Senators. During the Senate debate, Senator Daniel Brewster (D., Md.) asked: "So my question is whether there is anything in the resolution which would authorize, or recommend, or approve the landing of large American armies in Vietnam or in China?" Replied Senator J. William Fulbright (D., Ark.), floor manager of the resolution and Chairman of the Senate Foreign Relations Committee:

"There is nothing in the resolution, as I read it, that contemplates it. I agree with the Senator that that is the last thing we would want to do. However, the language of the resolution would not prevent it. It would authorize whatever the Commander in Chief feels is necessary. . . . Speaking for my own committee, everyone I have heard has said that the last thing we want to do is to become involved in a land war in Asia; that our power is sea and air. . . ."

The reply did not satisfy the Senate. Senator John Sherman Cooper (R., Ky.) went more directly to the heart of the issue. He engaged Senator Fulbright in a lengthy colloquy, part of which follows:

Senator Cooper: "The second section of the resolution goes, as the Senator said, to steps the President might take concerning the parties to the Southeast Asia Collective Defense Treaty and the countries under the protocol—which are, of course, Laos, Cambodia, and South Vietnam. The Senator will remember that the SEATO Treaty, in article IV, provides that in the event an armed attack is made upon a party to the Southeast Asia Collective Defense Treaty, or upon one of the protocol states such as South Vietnam, the parties to the treaty, one of whom is the United States, would then take such action as might be appropriate, after resorting to their constitutional processes. I assume that would mean, in the case of the United States, that Congress would be asked to grant the authority to act."

Senator Fulbright: "I think that is correct."

Senator Cooper: "Then, looking ahead, if the President decided that it was necessary to use such force as could lead into war, we will give that authority by this resolution?"

Senator Fulbright: "That is the way I would interpret it. . . ."

Senator Cooper: "I ask these questions because it is well for the country and all of us to know what is being undertaken. . . .

"Under section 2, are we are now providing the President, if he determines it necessary, the authority to attack cities and ports in North Vietnam, not primarily to prevent an attack upon our forces but, as he might see fit, to prevent any further aggression against South-Vietnam?"

Senator Fulbright: "One of the reasons for the procedure provided in this joint resolution, and also in the Formosa and Middle East instances is in response, let us say, to the new developments in the field of warfare. . . .

"Under modern conditions of warfare . . . it is necessary to anticipate what may occur. Things move so rapidly that this is the way in which we must respond to the new developments. That is why this provision is necessary or important. Does the Senator agree with me that this is so?"

Senator Cooper: "Yes, warfare today is different. Time is of the essence. But the power provided the President in section 2 is great.

Senator Fulbright: "This provision is intended to give clearance to the President to use his discretion. We all hope and believe that the President will not use this discretion arbitrarily or irresponsibly. We know that he is accustomed to consulting with the Joint Chiefs of Staff and with congressional leaders. But he does not have to do that."

Senator Cooper: "I understand, and believe that the President will use this vast power with judgment."

Senator Fulbright: "He intends to do it, and he has done it. . . ."

Senator Fulbright: "I have no doubt that the President will consult with Congress in case a major change in present policy becomes necessary."

Senator Cooper: ". . . I know it is understood and agreed that in the defense of our own ships and forces any action we might take to repel attacks could lead to war, if the Vietnamese or the Chinese Communists continued to engage in attacks against our forces. I hope they will be deterred by the prompt action of the President.

"We accept this first duty of security and honor. But I would feel untrue to my own convictions if I did not say that a different situation obtains with respect to South Vietnam. I know that a progression of events for 10 years has carried us to this crisis. Ten years have passed and perhaps the events are inevitable now, no one can tell. But as long as there is hope and the possibility of avoiding with honor a war in southeast Asia—a conflagration which, I must say, could lead into war with Communist China, and perhaps to a third world war with consequences one can scarcely contemplate today—I hope the President will use his power wisely with respect to our commitments in South Vietnam, and that he will use all other honorable means which may be available, such as consultations in the United Nations, and even with the Geneva powers.

"We have confidence in the President and in his good judgment. But I believe we have the obligation of understanding fully that there is a distinction between defending our own forces, and taking offensive measures in South Vietnam which could lead progressively to a third world war."

Perhaps the most often repeated statement during debate on the resolution was that the United States should not get bogged down in a land war in Asia. There were equally as many assurances that this was not contemplated.

Yet it was made quite clear that Section 2 of the resolution did in fact authorize the President to send land armies into Vietnam and also to bomb North Vietnam.

Certainly, from their colloquy, both Senator Cooper and Senator Fulbright were firm in their own minds that the resolution did authorize whatever actions the President might see fit to take. If this is the correct interpretation, then it would appear the President is on firm ground when he states—as he has so often since stated—that later commitments of U. S. ground forces to combat as well as the bombings of North Vietnam were authorized by Congress.

Congress drew some assurance from its assumption in 1964 that such a contingency was remote and that the President, being a man of "good judgment," would not act rashly, would use his power cautiously, would always consult Congress as well as the U. N. and the Geneva powers.

The President was to give Congress ample ground for this belief during 1964. During the entire presidential election campaign he repeatedly assured the American people he was not in office to engage in such a massive land war or to take rash actions.

During the debate on the resolution, Senator Thruston B. Morton summarized the feelings of many Republicans in Congress when he said, "I believe Congress should speak loud and clear and make it plain to any would-be aggressor that we intend to stand here. If we make that clear we will avoid war, and not have to land vast armies on the shores of Asia." The President found the resolution spoke loudly enough and clearly enough so that he signed it on August 11.

But this was an election year. And the very next day, August 12, the President was to dull the sound and blur the clarity of the resolution—and his own intentions—with a campaign speech to the Bar Association in New York. He spoke sorrowfully of those who were "eager to enlarge the conflict" and then added:

"They call upon us to supply American boys to do the job that Asian boys should do. They ask us to take reckless action which might risk the lives of millions and engulf much of Asia and certainly threaten the peace of the entire world. Moreover such action would offer no solution at all to the real problem of Vietnam."

This thesis, that American boys were not to be sent half-way around the world to do the job Asian boys should be doing, was repeated in an Akron, Ohio, speech on October 21.

This was the President's campaign reassurance to the American people; it may also have contributed to the Communist miscalculation as to American intentions in Vietnam.

Election Year Bargain Budget. Reinforcing Congress' belief that the U. S. commitment in Vietnam would be limited, new obligational authority sought for defense had dropped from $48.1 billion in fiscal 1963, to $47.2 billion in fiscal 1964.

A further decline had been registered in fiscal 1965 when defense new obligation authority (requested in January 1964) amounted to only $46.8 billion. In short, the election year defense requests did not reflect the realities of fighting then going on.

By March 1964, newspaper accounts described Vietnamese reluctance to take U. S. military advice and described the difficulties we were facing in getting Vietnamese troops to fight. On April 25 the Associated Press reported that in the first four and a half months of 1964, 324 American servicemen had become battle casualties.

Beginning in May, with American forces already in combat, reports of serious shortages were verified, making necessary the use of dangerously obsolete equipment. On May 15th Rep. Carl Vinson, then Chairman of the House Armed Services Committee, announced he would call Secretary McNamara for a closed session in regard to a full-scale investigation of the use of obsolete military equipment in Vietnam.

The distressing series of events led Senator Everett McKinley Dirksen to declare on May 27th: "While the Johnson administration falters in indecision, the United States is a party to another treadmill conflict . . ."

By July 1964 the war was costing the United States $1.5 million a day. Announced troop strength in Vietnam had climbed to 18,000.

The administration found it necessary to request a $700 million defense supplemental appropriation specifically for the war in Vietnam, the first in a chain of afterthought supplementals to follow.

Yet total U. S. troop strength levels consistently failed to reflect the escalation of conflict in Vietnam. On June 30, 1962, total active duty military personnel numbered 2,807,819. On June 30, 1963, troop strength was down to 2,699,677 and the next year, on June 30, 1964, down a third time to 2,687,409. By June 30, 1965, after five years of steadily increasing U. S. commitment in Vietnam, total active duty U. S. military personnel had further declined to 2,655,389.

President Johnson's refusal to allow budget requests to follow, even remotely, the actual course of events in Vietnam was to plague the military up to the fiscal 1968 budget. For instance, in fiscal 1966 his initial defense spending request was only $46.8 billion, but once again a supplemental appropriation of $13.1 billion was required later in the year.

Again, in fiscal 1967, although the main defense appropriation jumped approximately $11.2 billion, a supplemental appropriation of $12.2 billion was requested and received later in the year.

The effect on military procurement—particularly the so-called "long leadtime" items requiring commitment well in advance of actual delivery—was devastating from 1963 through 1966.

Korea—The Forgotten Lesson. To a frightening degree, these events paralleled the mistakes made over a decade earlier by another Democratic administration in Korea. Said President Johnson in his January 1967 Budget Message to Congress:

"A year ago we were in the midst of a rapid buildup of our forces in Vietnam. Rather than submit a budget to the Congress based on highly uncertain estimates, I requested funds sufficient to finance the conflict through fiscal year 1967. At the present time the situation is different. While unforeseen events can upset the most careful estimate, we are in a much better position to determine our future requirements in Vietnam. As a consequence, my 1968 budget provides for those requirements on a continuing basis, including the possibility of an extension of combat beyond the end of the fiscal year."

Said the Senate Preparedness Investigation Subcommittee 14 years earlier, in May 1953:

"To touch specifically on the budgetary guidelines, it has been

testified that the planners could not plan properly for the Korean
War because one of the assumptions was that it would be over by
the beginning of the fiscal year which was being planned. Budget
requests were based on the amount of ammo used plus the replacement of reserve stocks with no thought that the War would continue
for a longer period of time.

"In hindsight this is a most unrealistic policy or assumption. It
may well have had an adverse effect on our military planners. We
know that applied to the Korean ammunition program, an adverse
effect occurred somewhere because no substantial quantity of ammunition was produced, and this was responsible for depleting our exist-
ing stocks. This is the result of partial mobilization."

Finally, in 1967, Mr. McNamara was to admit:

"Since we can now project our requirements for the conflict in
Southeast Asia with far greater confidence than last year, we have
changed our basic approach in preparing the FY 1967 Supplemental
as well as the FY 1968 Budget. Sufficient funds are being requested
in both the FY 1967 Supplemental and the FY 1968 Budget to protect
the production leadtime. . . ."

In belated recognition of this fact, the initial Defense Budget
request this year is fully $75 billion.

Peace Proposals—1964. After President Kennedy's assassination,
repeated newspaper stories told of attempts by U. N. Secretary General U Thant to arrange for some sort of peace negotiations between
Hanoi and Washington. Their authenticity was denied by the Johnson administration.

Today we know that Mr. Thant, in September 1964, made a serious
proposal to Hanoi and Washington that they secretly send representatives to Rangoon, Burma to discuss the Vietnam war. Hanoi accepted
the proposal yet Washington turned it down.

According to the late Adlai Stevenson, the Johnson administration
refused to discuss peace in Vietnam with Hanoi because of the possible effect on the 1964 elections.

Secretary Thant agreed to wait. After President Johnson's overwhelming reelection, he again made the proposal. Hanoi again agreed
but the Johnson administration, through Secretary McNamara, once
again refused.

When *The New York Times* on March 9, 1965 reported that U
Thant had undertaken to arrange for such negotiations, Mr. Johnson's

State Department denied it had in fact rejected Thant's proposals.

Only after Eric Sevareid published his article in the November 30, 1965, *Look* concerning the late U. N. Ambassador Adlai Stevenson, including Stevenson's revelations about the Thant mission, did the State Department at long last admit to the existence of the Thant proposal and that it had been rejected.

This episode, when added to the host of other incidents, utterances, misleading statements, half-truths, outright untruths, emphasizes the hallmark of the Johnson administration in the conduct of the Vietnam war—a complete lack of candor.

The Americanization of the War. President John Kennedy once remarked the war in Vietnam could be won only so long as it was their war. If it were ever converted into a white man's war, we would lose as the French had lost a decade earlier. In the French period, Paris had some 5,000 to 7,000 administrators, plus the French colonials, in Vietnam. Their troop commitment reached 272,000.

Today the United States has roughly 500,000 military men in Southeast Asia, plus about 30,000 American civilians, with more of each to come, and with Americans doing most of the fighting.

How did this war become Americanized? As the record has shown, a qualitative shift in the American commitment in 1961—from arms, money, and advisors to armed combat troops—set the stage for increased United States involvement. It also set the stage for the next shift in our commitment, this time a quantitative change.

On February 7, 1965, eight Americans were killed, 62 wounded in a guerrilla attack by the Viet Cong. President Johnson promptly ordered the Air Force into a retaliatory attack on targets in North Vietnam. Soviet Prime Minister Kosygin was in Hanoi at the time of the first bombing attack.

Correspondents on the scene have speculated Kosygin had gone to Hanoi on a mission to wean North Vietnam away from Peking. The Chinese Communists had not given Hanoi as much material support as promised. Kosygin was in Hanoi to promise Ho Chi Minh more supplies and equipment.

The bombing, when it came, gave the Soviet Union its "reason"—for public consumption, at least—for making such an offer. On February 9, Kosygin made his first public announcement of stepped-up Soviet support for the Hanoi regime.

Each of the first three raids, we carefully notified Moscow, were in retaliation for specific attacks against American military personnel in South Vietnam.

Bombing And Troops—Up And Up. During this period the military situation in South Vietnam was deteriorating badly. Vietnamese army units were being defeated daily; the Vietnamese army was losing a battalion a week; district capitals were falling weekly; village strongpoints were being overrun nightly.

Within this framework the President stepped up the bombing of North Vietnam, no longer as retaliatory raids but as an effort to break the supply route to the South which Ho was using to supply the Viet Cong. American military strength in South Vietnam began to climb dramatically; by mid-1965 we had 53,000 ground troops in Vietnam and by year's end over 200,000.

The escalation continued through 1966. Our bombings, formerly tactical—to interdict supply routes—were now strategic, as well, aimed at whatever steel mills, power plants, industrial complexes existed. By spring of 1967, the United States had committed 500,000 men to a land war in Asia and was spending, for that conflict alone, one-fifth of its entire national budget.

In casualties, there are over 9,000 Americans dead; 50,000 wounded. We have lost over 1,200 airplanes and nearly 800 helicopters.

Yet at the beginning of April 1967, the United States and South Vietnamese were able to claim control over fewer villages and hamlets than in 1962.

Administration Policy. In 1961 the State Department issued a white paper on Vietnam which emphasized the indigenous nature of the conflict. It said in part:

"The basic pattern of Viet Cong (Vietnamese Communist) activity is not new, of course. It operated, with minor variations, in China, and Mao Tse-tung's theories on the conduct of guerrilla warfare are known to every Viet Cong agent and cadre. *Most of the same methods were used in Malaya, in Greece, in the Philippines, in Cuba, and in Laos. If there is anything peculiar to the Vietnam situation, it is that the country is divided and one-half provides a safe sanctuary from which subversion in the other half is directed and supported with both personnel and materiel."*

By 1965 the indigenous character of the Viet Cong was being played down in favor of the new theme; that is, aggression from the north.

Said the 1965 State Department white paper on Vietnam, in part:

"The war in Vietnam is a new kind of war, a fact as yet poorly understood in most parts of the world. Much of the confusion that prevails in the thinking of many people, and even many governments, stems from this basic misunderstanding. For in Vietnam a totally new brand of aggression has been loosed against an independent people who want to make their own way in peace and freedom.

"Vietnam is *not* another Greece, where indigenous guerrilla forces used friendly neighboring territory as a sanctuary. [Emphasis State's own].

"Vietnam is *not* another Malaya, where Communist guerrillas were, for the most part, physically distinguishable from the peaceful majority they sought to control.

"Vietnam is *not* another Philippines, where Communist guerrillas were physically separated from the source of their moral and physical support."

Perhaps the State Department was correct in its new assessment of the nature of the war. Perhaps, too, the increased North Vietnamese involvement was to match increased U. S. commitment to battle.

Preconditions To Negotiations. This second white paper was issued during a three-week lull between the first retaliatory air raids on North Vietnam in 1965 and the commencement of sustained bombing. During this lull, U Thant, recognizing the possibility of retaliation turning into open warfare, approached Hanoi and Washington with a renewed plea for negotiations.

The Johnson administration at this point laid down what seemed to be two basic preconditions to peace negotiations: (1) That Hanoi accept South Vietnam as a separate and independent state. (2) That Hanoi agree to pull all forces out of the South.

Meanwhile, a separate appeal had come from the conference of 17 so-called nonaligned nations meeting at Belgrade asking Hanoi to negotiate. Both appeals—Thant's and nonaligned nations'—were dismissed by Hanoi on grounds the United States had already rejected any negotiations on a "no-preconditions" basis.

Johnson Position Hardens. In retrospect, it is clear the Johnson administration did not wish to negotiate during this period. The Saigon government controlled barely 20 percent of South Vietnam. Its generals made no bones of the fact they were losing to the Viet Cong.

To come to the bargaining table in hopes of salvaging an independent South Vietnam would be asking the impossible. In 1954, at Geneva, Ho Chi Minh had agreed to relinquish the area of Vietnam south of the 17th parallel in return for nationwide elections in 1956, elections which failed to materialize. For the U. S. to hope for similar concessions in 1965 was unrealistic.

In commenting on the President's attitude toward negotiation at this time, Senator Albert Gore (D., Tenn.) said: "We know that at one time President Johnson opposed negotiation. He was very much opposed to negotiation or a negotiated settlement at the time I suggested more than a year ago. . . . Fortunately at his speech at Johns Hopkins [in April 1965], he changed his strategy and came to what I think was a far more realistic defensible, feasible position."

President Johnson added to the confusion surrounding a negotiated settlement when, on March 25, 1965, he said, "We seek no more than a return to the essentials of the agreements of 1954—a reliable agreement to guarantee the independence and security of all in Southeast Asia."

Did the President indeed wish to return to the essentials of the 1954 Geneva Agreement? To hold nationwide elections in Vietnam as provided for at Geneva? To withdraw all foreign troops as provided for at Geneva? To reunite North and South Vietnam as provided for at Geneva? Or was the U. S. position really the one stated by Dean Rusk February 25, 1965, i.e. that Hanoi must accept South Vietnam as a separate, independent state?

Again, contradiction within the welter of statements coming from the Johnson administration confuses not only Americans, but allies, bystanders and enemy alike. If a policy of deliberate obfuscation was desired, Mr. Rusk and Mr. Johnson succeeded. Clearly, too many "official" statements have been made by too many different officials, shaped and adapted to the wants of too many different audiences.

On April 13, 1965, Hanoi also hardened its position, laying down four principal points:

"1. Recognition of the basic national rights of the Viet Nam people: peace, independence, sovereignty, unity and territorial integrity.

"2. Pending peaceful reunification of Viet Nam, while Viet Nam is still temporarily divided into two zones, the military provisions of the 1954 Geneva agreements on Viet Nam must be strictly respected; the two zones must refrain from joining any military alliance with foreign countries, there must be no foreign military bases, troops and military personnel in their respective territory.

"3. The internal affairs of South Vietnam must be settled by the South Vietnamese people themselves, in accordance with the program of the South Vietnam National Front for Liberation [Viet Cong], without any foreign interference.

"4. The peaceful reunification of Viet Nam is to be settled by the Vietnamese people in both zones, without any foreign interference."

Present Political Situation. The South Vietnamese Constituent Assembly in March 1967, adopted a new constitution for the Republic. It was promptly approved by the ruling junta of Marshal Ky. The constitution provides for free elections throughout South Vietnam and on the surface seems to provide some hope for stability and political progress.

However, with the Viet Cong controlling at least 50 percent of the territory, and 40 percent of the population—and even more when the sun is down—the significance of the elections seems problematical. Elections for President are scheduled September 1, 1967.

It is also problematic as to how freely a newly-elected government can operate. The military, to date, has provided the most cohesive force in Vietnam, at least from our viewpoint. It can be assumed they will let go of the reins of power reluctantly, constitution or no constitution. The problem, however, is not simply the military in Saigon, according to seasoned Southeast Asia reporter, Marvin L. Stone, in his article "Vietnam—A Hopeless War?", in *U. S. News and World Report* for Dec. 5, 1966:

"At the top, it is a Government of power blocs and factionalism, in the French tradition. Leaders in Saigon are preoccupied fighting to keep their grasp on power.

"At just about every level below the top it is a Government of local fiefs, run by entrenched military sycophants or petty underpaid civil-service officials."

This, says Stone, means that District or Province chiefs in the countryside buy their jobs and impose their own "unofficial" forms of taxation to make a profit. The peasant has no place to turn for relief. Adds Stone:

". . . Saigon's land-reform program, so vital to the aspirations of peasants, has never really been put in motion. In the secure areas, tenant farmers—that means 70 per cent of all farmers in the Delta—

still are forced to pay up to 50 per cent and more of their rice crops to absentee landlords who have absolutely no obligation in return. A law on the books since 1955 sets the limit at 25 per cent.

"Americans here insist that no progress will be made so long as the men at the top in Saigon are members of mandarin families, or allied with families which have vested interests in land that they have no intention of relinquishing."

1965-1966 Peace Feelers. The year 1965 marks the beginning of an enormous number of proposals from all over the globe for peaceful negotiations. They can be summarized as follows:

• Reconvening the 1954 Geneva Conference to effect a cease fire and eventual peace.

• Direct negotiations between Washington and Hanoi.

• A mediation effort through U Thant.

• Resort to the U. N. General Assembly or Security Council as mediators.

• Negotiations between Saigon and Hanoi.

• Negotiations to achieve a neutral federation of Laos, Cambodia, and South Vietnam.

• Negotiations between Saigon and the NLF-Viet Cong with Hanoi and Washington backstopping each side.

• Negotiations between Saigon, Hanoi, and the NLF with a neutral nation acting as chairman.

• Informal discussions between Hanoi and Washington in a neutral country to determine whether any grounds for formal negotiations exist.

It is physically impossible to compare the texts of each of the proposals and note all the differences, all the conditions, whether they are factual, semantic, or mere nuance. Nor can each such proposal be detailed. For these reasons, this study is confined to the last known U. S. position, contained in President Johnson's letter to Ho Chi Minh of February 1967, and in the exchange between U. N. Secretary General U Thant and Mr. Johnson.

Previous administration utterances—at Johns Hopkins in 1965, the Hawaii Conference of December 1965, the Manila Conference of 1966 and the Guam Conference of 1967—while significant, must be considered in the context of domestic American politics, in the context of current world opinion, and in the context of the actual military situation in Vietnam at the particular time they were issued.

Thus the present position of Mr. Johnson and his advisors is the only truly useful benchmark in this spring of 1967. It is, as best as can be judged, contained in the texts of a letter from President Johnson to President Ho Chi Minh, dated February 2, 1967, and in the North Vietnamese leader's reply, dated February 15, 1967, and translated from the French in Washington:

President Johnson's letter of February 2, 1967, to Ho Chi Minh states:

"I am writing to you in the hope that the conflict in Vietnam can be brought to an end. That conflict has already taken a heavy toll— in lives lost, in wounds inflicted, in property destroyed and in simple human misery. If we fail to find a just and peaceful solution, history will judge us harshly.

"Therefore, I believe that we both have a heavy obligation to seek earnestly the path to peace. It is in response to that obligation that I am writing directly to you.

"We have tried over the past several years, in a variety of ways and through a number of channels, to convey to you and your colleagues our desire to achieve a peaceful settlement. For whatever reasons, these efforts have not achieved any results.

"It may be that our thoughts and yours, our attitudes and yours, have been distorted or misinterpreted as they passed through these various channels. Certainly that is always a danger in indirect communication.

"There is one good way to overcome this problem and to move forward in search for a peaceful settlement. That is for us to arrange for direct talks between trusted representatives in a secure setting and away from the glare of publicity. Such talks should not be used as a propaganda exercise, but should be a serious effort to find a workable and mutually acceptable solution.

"In the past two weeks, I have noted public statements by representatives of your Government suggesting that you would be prepared to enter into direct bilateral talks with representatives of the U. S. Government, provided that we ceased "unconditionally" and permanently our bombing operations against your country and all military actions again it. In the last day, serious and responsible parties have assured us indirectly that this is in fact your proposal.

"Let me frankly state that I see two great difficulties with this proposal. In view of your public position, such action on our part would inevitably produce worldwide speculation that discussions were under way and would impair the privacy and secrecy of those discussions. Secondly, there would inevitably be grave concern on our part whether your Government would make use of such action by us to improve its military position.

"With these problems in mind, I am prepared to move even further toward an ending of hostilities than your Government has proposed in either public statements or through private diplomatic channels. I am prepared to order a cessation of bombing against your country and the stopping of further augmentation of United States forces in South Vietnam as soon as I am assured that infiltration into South Vietnam by land and by sea has stopped. These acts of restraint on both sides would, I believe, make it possible for us to conduct serious and private discussions leading toward an early peace.

"I make this proposal to you now with a specific sense of urgency arising from the imminent new year holidays in Vietnam. If you are able to accept this proposal I see no reason why it could not take effect at the end of the new year, or Tet, holidays. The proposal I have made would be greatly strengthened if your military authorities and those of the Government of South Vietnam could promptly negotiate an extension of the Tet truce.

"As to the site of the bilateral discussions I propose, there are several possibilities. We could, for example, have our representatives meet in Moscow where contacts have already occurred. They could meet in some other country such as Burma. You may have other arrangements or sites in mind, and I would try to meet your suggestions.

"The important thing is to end a conflict that has brought burdens to both our peoples, and above all to the people of South Vietnam. If you have any thoughts about the actions I propose, it would be most important that I receive them as soon as possible.

Ho Chi Minh's reply of February 15, 1967, to President Johnson's letter of February 2nd states:

"On 10 February 1967, I received your message. This is my reply.

"Vietnam is thousands of miles away from the United States. The Vietnamese people have never done any harm to the United States. But contrary to the pledges made by its representative at the 1954 Geneva conference, the U.S. Government has ceaselessly intervened in Vietnam; it has unleashed and intensified the war of aggression in South Vietnam with a view to prolonging the partition of Vietnam and turning South Vietnam into a neocolony and a military base of the United States. For over two years now, the U. S. Government has with its air and naval forces carried the war to the Democratic Republic of Vietnam, an independent and sovereign country.

"The U. S. Government has committed war crimes, crimes against peace and against mankind. In South Vietnam, half a million U. S. and satellite troops have resorted to the most inhuman weapons and the most barbarous methods of warfare, such as napalm, toxic chemicals and gases, to massacre our compatriots, destroy crops and raze villages to the ground.

"In North Vietnam, thousands of U. S. aircraft have dropped hundreds of thousands of tons of bombs, destroying towns, villages, factories, roads, bridges, dikes, dams and even churches, pagodas, hospitals, schools. In your message, you apparently deplored the sufferings and destructions in Vietnam. May I ask you: Who has perpetrated these monstrous crimes? It is the U. S. and satellite troops. The U. S. Government is entirely responsible for the extremely serious situation in Vietnam.

"The U. S. war of aggression against the Vietnamese people constitutes a challenge to the countries of the Socialist camp, a threat to the national independence movement and a serious danger to peace in Asia and the world.

"The Vietnamese people deeply love independence, freedom and peace. But in the face of the U. S. aggression, they have risen up, united as one man. Fearless of sacrifices and hardships, they are determined to carry on their resistance until they have won genuine independence and freedom and true peace. Our just cause enjoys strong sympathy and support from the peoples of the whole world, including broad sections of the American people.

"The U. S. Government has unleashed the war of aggression in Vietnam. It must cease this aggression. That is the only way to the restoration of peace. The U. S. Government must stop definitely and unconditionally its bombing raids and all other acts of war against the Democratic Republic of Vietnam, withdraw from South Vietnam all U. S. and satellite troops, and let the Vietnamese people settle themselves their own affairs. Such [is the basic] content of the four-point stand of the Government of the D.R.V., which embodies the essential principles and provisions of the 1954 Geneva agreements on Vietnam. It is the basis of a correct political solution to the Vietnam problem.

"In your message, you suggested direct talks between the D.R.V. and the United States. If the U. S. Government really wants these talks, it must first of all stop unconditionally its bombing raids and all other acts of war against the D.R.V. It is only after the unconditional cessation of the U. S. bombing raids and all other acts of war against the D.R.V. that the D.R.V. and the United States would enter into talks and discuss questions concerning the two sides.

"The Vietnamese people will never submit to force, they will never accept talks under the threat of bombs.

"Our cause is absolutely just. It is to be hoped that the U. S. Government will act in accordance with reason."

The second expression of position is contained in statements of U. N. Secretary General U Thant in March 1967.

On March 28th U Thant called a news conference and presented a new three-point peace formula that he had circulated secretly in mid-March. Mr. U Thant's formula was this:

First, a "general standstill truce . . . a halt to all military activities by all sides."

Second, preliminary talks between the United States and North Vietnam, attended either by Britain and the Soviet Union, as co-chairmen of the 1954 Geneva Conference on Vietnam, and/or Canada, India, and Poland, as the International Control Commission for Vietnam.

Third, reconvening the Geneva Conference with both the South Vietnamese Government and the Viet Cong as participants.

The day before, Hanoi radio had broadcast U Thant's proposals, pointedly rebuffing United Nation's "interference" in Vietnam. U Thant held out hope that Hanoi had not "categorically" turned him down, while U. S. Secretary of State Dean Rusk treated Hanoi's negative response as a fatal blow to the Thant initiative.

Yet, as Washington congratulated itself on its good fortune in finding itself squarely in agreement with the Secretary General of the U.N., U Thant had begun to slide back to his previous position that the U. S. must stop bombing North Vietnam as a necessary precondition to negotiations.

Meanwhile, Saigon was reported to be in agreement in principle with the U Thant three-point proposal, but displeased at being precluded from preliminary talks and "being treated like a puppet."

Thereafter, Washington qualified its acceptance of the same three-point proposal by saying "it is essential" to work out the details of the military cease-fire in advance.

And there the matter would seem to rest.

4

CONCLUSION

Obviously, there is a great amount of information to which only Mr. Johnson and his advisors have access. A review such as this must perforce rely on materials that have been made public by the administration, or are obtainable from other public sources.

One other observation is necessary. Deep currents, Asian in origin, hold enormous sway over events in Vietnam yet cannot be adequately treated in a brief political history. A list of such currents is large, and would include the observation that Vietnam is basically Buddhist and Confucian, both ethical religions without a personal god. Thus, Asiatic communism as espoused by Asiatics can masquerade as an ally in the older, more familiar struggle against Western theism, Western colonialism, and Western capitalism.

Such a list would necessarily include also the tragic involvement of Diem's brother Nhu with opium; the profound effect the writings of an obscure French Catholic philosopher, Emmanuel Mounier, was to have on Nhu and in turn on his lonely, celibate brother, Diem; the fact that Nhu and Diem translated Mounier's "personnalisme" ethic into a secret, authoritarian organization, the "Can Lao" (Personalist Labor Revolutionary Party), to control all aspects of government and society in South Vietnam, thereby tragically destroying the coalition they had put together in 1954-55; even the distaste of individual Vietnamese in thousands of daily contacts at levels high and low for open, frank, Western speech compared to their own fluid, often subtle, conversational forms. These accidents of culture, history, and geography, for better or for worse, carry equally as much weight in the Vietnamese conflict today as, say, the effective fire power of the 7th fleet on a given day.

In a larger sense much more can be cited to confound the best of minds in resolving the Vietnamese conflict. The West divides good and evil, and thinks that evil can be conquered. Yet in Asia, a man is generally capable of believing that something is simultaneously good and bad, right and wrong, black and white, in such a manner as to render most difficult real understanding by the Western mentality.

Just as difficult to comprehend are the "politics" of the Buddhists, or the meaning of their proposals for a peaceful, independent Vietnam; we dismiss them as visionary or unrealistic, yet they may be more acceptable and understandable to the South Vietnamese — after 27 years of warfare — than anything we propose in our Western political terminology.

In short, we Americans cannot simply go to Asia, wipe the slate clean, and say to them, "This is how it shall be." The Vietnamese have their own view of nationalism, quite different from ours, the Vietnamese Communists identify with it, and it renders our involvement immeasurably difficult.

Further Decisions. Does the Republican Party serve America best by saying that politics stops at the water's edge? That we must rally behind the President? Does bipartisanship mean that Democratic mistakes are Republican responsibilities?

Republicans — for two decades — have believed the United States must not become involved in a land war on the Asian continent. We are so involved today.

Republicans have believed that no American military intervention should be unilateral. Our commitment today in Vietnam is primarily unilateral.

Republicans, in 1954, made a limited commitment to the South Vietnam Government. Under the Democrats, our commitment has become open-ended.

Before making any further decisions to support or differ with the President, Republicans might agree to seek hard, realistic answers to two basic questions:

1. What precisely is our national interest in Thailand, Cambodia, Vietnam, and Laos?

2. To what further lengths are we prepared to go in support of this interest?

APPENDIX I

TROOP STRENGTH

	AMERICAN	A.R.V.N.[1]	VIET CONG[2]
1961	3,164	338,000	63,400
1962	9,865	467,000	79,000
1963	16,500	525,000	91,700
1964	23,000	559,500	103,000
1965	181,000	679,000	230,000
1966	389,000	671,000	280,000
1967	430,000 [3]	650,000 [3]	287,000 [3]

1. Source, 1961-1966: Department of Defense through United States Senate Armed Services Committee; 1967: *Washington Post*, April 14, 1967.
2. South Vietnam Communists, strength in the south. Source, 1961-1966: Department of Defense through United States Senate Armed Services Committee; 1967: *Washington Post*, April 14, 1967.

   (Unable to obtain official estimates as to total number of regular North Vietnam troops in south.)
3. As of April 1, 1967.

Appendix II

CASUALTIES

	Americans Killed[1]	A.R.V.N. Killed[2]	Enemy Killed[3]
1960		2,200	5,669
1961	} 42	4,000	12,133
1962		4,400	21,158
1963	78	5,700	20,575
1964	147	7,500	16,785
1965	1,369	11,000	35,436
1966	5,008	9,400	55,524
1967	2,434[5]	2,954[4]	25,773[4]
Total	9,078	47,154	193,053

1. In hostile action. Source: Department of Defense.
2. Source, 1960-1966: Department of Defense through United States Senate Armed Services Committee; 1967: *Washington Post,* compiled from news dispatches.
3. Source: *Washington Post,* April 14, 1967.
4. As of April 1, 1967.
5. As of April 15, 1967.

Appendix III

CASUALTIES[1]

(Wounded and Non-combat Dead)

	AMERICANS DEAD	AMERICANS WOUNDED
1961	23	81
1962		
1963	36	411
1964	48	1,039
1965	359	6,114
1966	1,045	30,093
1967	398[2]	16,350[2]
Total................................	1,909	54,088

1. Source: Department of Defense.

2. As of April 15, 1967.

Appendix IV

	Enemy Captured [1]	Enemy Defections [2]
1961	6,200	
1962	5,500	
1963	4,000	
1964	4,200	11,000
1965	6,000	5,500
1966	10,000	20,000
1967	1,000 [3]	8,000 [4]
Total	36,826	44,500

1. Source, 1961-1966: Department of Defense through United States Senate Armed Services Committee; 1967: *Washington Post,* April 14, 1967.

2. Source: Department of Defense through United States Senate Armed Services Committee.

3. January 1967 only.

4. As of April 1, 1967.

Recent Important Books

CRISIS DIPLOMACY. By D. A. Graber. A history of U.S. intervention policies and practices. Published in coperation with the University of Chicago Center for Study of American Foreign Policy. $6.75

CHINA, VIETNAM AND THE UNITED STATES. Highlights of the hearings of the Senate Foreign Relations Committee — including statements by J. William Fulbright, George Kennan, James Gavin, Maxwell Taylor, and others. $2.95

VIETNAM AND THE UNITED STATES. By Hans J. Morgenthau. A leading critic of American policies presents his views. Contains new material as well as recent articles. $2.00

AMERICA'S VIETNAM POLICY. By Edward Herman and Richard Du Boff. A carefully documented analysis of the credibility of official claims and representations. $2.00

THAILAND AND THE UNITED STATES. By Frank C. Darling. A sophisticated critique of diplomatic and political relationships since World War II. $6.00

WASHINGTON EXPOSE. By Jack Anderson. A no-holds-barred book by Drew Pearson's associate. Jam-packed with hard facts and forthright comments. Profusely ilustrated with surprising exhibits. $6.00

THE LOBBYISTS. By James Deakin. A readable, authoritative and revealing book by a Washington reporter of St. Louis Post-Dispatch. $6.00

THE POLITICS OF RESEARCH. By Richard J. Barber. A bold appraisal of practices and problems arising out of publicly financed undertakings in the United States. $4.50

PROPAGANDA COMES OF AGE. By Michael Choukas. A widely hailed examination of the techniques of public opinion manipulation. Foreword by Hadley Cantril. $6.00

A HISTORY OF SINO-RUSSIAN RELATIONS. By Tien-Fong Cheng. An authoritative work, critically oriented, by China's former Minister of Education. $6.00

Public Affairs Press, 419 New Jersey Ave., S.E., Washington, D. C.

H3660